1

Cover and Illustrations by Robert Oldham.
Independently published.

ISBN 9798398821130

Characters in this book are:

The Topplelites

Grandad Joe Topplelite
Charlie Topplelite
Betty Topplelite
Tina Topplelite
Jimmy Topplelite

The Hornites

King Horn
Morton the Snake
Drax and Obo
Hornet
Ox

Other Characters

Birdy Williams
Captain Scampi
The Wise Tree

Chapter Contents

Meet the Topplelites

It was a beautiful day in Toppleland and the sun was beaming down on the Topplelite family who were busy working in the Topplefruit forest picking fruit, this was the sort of place where everyone knew each other and life in general is very peaceful, everyone was happy with their lives and loved living in place of such natural beauty with its rolling hills and endless woodlands that surrounded the homes of everyone living there, the birds were singing and everyone in the land going about their business.

To help you through the adventure I have drawn you a map to help you navigate your way around the land, I'm nice to you aren't I. Basically from what you've read so far everything sounds perfect, well it would be if

it wasn't for one problem and it comes in the shape of King Horn, he lives in Horn Castle which is to the north of Toppleland, you may have already noticed this on the map as it does stick out a bit in such a beautiful country setting, generally he has nothing to do with any of the Topplefolk, he keeps himself locked away in his castle minding his own business. The castle is located on the top of a huge hill

surrounded by dense woodland which is mostly full of dead trees and thorny bramble bushes.

Jimmy Topplelite was helping his Mum and Dad pick fruits in Topplefruit Forest, he helped by picking and packing the fruits into boxes ready for collection by the customers. I'll introduce you to the family there's Jimmy's Dad, Charlie, his Mum, Betty, and his sister, Tina,

they all live in a mushroom shaped house west of Topplefruit forest and they also own a fruit sorting business in the centre of the forest.

The Topple family have made their living this way for many generations and one day they hope to expand the business to bigger premises and send their delicious fruits to customers all over the world, now that would be their ultimate dream.

Topplefruit Forest was known far and wide for growing Multi-coloured fruits, each coloured fruit has its own unique taste, these fruits are identified the same way you or I would tell an apple from an orange, the difference is that each tree can have up to eight different fruits on it. The family make their living from harvesting these fruits, they also trade and sell them to the locals as well as the neighbouring villages.

Jimmy had been collecting and packing the fruits for most of the morning and was about ready to leave to see his Grandad who had asked him over to show him his new invention.

Grandpa Joe Topplelite was the eldest of the Topplelite family and is a very enthusiastic inventor.

Jimmy waved goodbye to his family and left them to go to Grandads for the afternoon. What incredible invention had Grandad made now? Jimmy ran all the way to his Grandads house and hoped that one day he would be an inventor just like him.

Grandads New Boots

Grandad Joe lived in wishing forest and was getting his new invention ready to show his grandson Jimmy. He knew how much he loved to be the first to see his new inventions.

Jimmy was so excited, his run turned into a sprint to get him there even faster, when Jimmy reached Grandads, he was totally exhausted and stopped to catch his breath outside his house. Grandad's house was an unusual dome shaped building he designed and built himself, all his inventing was done

in his large fully equipped cellar.

Jimmy rang the doorbell and because

Jimmy was so excited the two minutes it

took Grandad to answer the doorbell

seemed like forever, the door opened and

there stood Grandad, the main

characteristic that stands out on him is his

huge grey beard that reached all the way to

his belly.

"Hello Jimmy, come on in and see my new

invention," Grandad said.

"I can't wait, Grandad, what is it?" Jimmy

replied.

"Come to my workshop and I'll show you!" said Grandad.

Jimmy followed his Grandad into his house through the lounge to a door that leads to his basement workshop, once inside Jimmy could see many machine parts and tools of all descriptions.

There on a workbench was what looked like a pair of modified brown walking boots surrounded by other attachments and many sketches and plans were stuck on the wall showing different aspects of the boots from the building of them to how the finished article would look.

Jimmy picked up the boots "Grandad are these your new invention?" Jimmy said eagerly.

"Yes Jimmy, they sure are, they are rocket powered boots and they are going to take me to far-off lands," Grandad answered eagerly.

"That's fantastic Grandad, when is the test flight?" Jimmy said excitedly.

"Well, there's no time like the present, let's head for the hills and try them out," Grandad replied.

"Whoopee let's go Grandad," Jimmy shouted.

So, Grandad put the rocket boots in a
holdall as well as some other necessities
and put them in the back of his van and both
Grandad and Jimmy headed for the hills.
Grandad stopped at Topplelite's family
home, their house was in the shape of a
mushroom, a smaller version of this house
was in Topplefruit forest and was used as a
fruit storing shed for the family business.
As not to interrupt the rest of the family who
were still busy in the forest, Grandad and
Jimmy cut through the forest behind the

house to get to the rolling hills of Toppleland where the test flight would take place. It seemed to be getting warmer by the minute, luckily there was a slight breeze that took the edge off the burning heat. The sun was glowing yellow and there wasn't a cloud in the sky, this certainly was a perfect day to test the Rocket boots.

Grandad emptied his large holdall and the contents inside were as follows,

Rocket boots checklist

1) A protective all in one suit

2) Two long fuel hoses

3) A pair of rocket powered boots

4) Two long trigger handles

5) A fuel canister

6) Safety goggles and some tasty cheese and pickle sandwiches all snugly fitted into his backpack.

Well... there's always time for a cheese and pickle sandwich isn't there?

Grandad put on the protective suit and lifted the heavy backpack onto his back, then he tied the boot laces with a double bow and pushed the excess laces in the boots, then he attached a trigger handles to each of the rocket boots and lastly fitted two fuel hoses from the fuel canister to each of the rocket boots. The rocket boots were cleverly put together and the best thing of all was the rocket boots were fuelled by the fruits found in Topplefruit forest, now that's what you call an invention, very eco-friendly, Grandad always thought about the planet when designing and building his gadgets and inventions, carbon zero all the way, protecting the planet was something he was very passionate about, Lastly, Grandad even put in a safety device which was concealed in the rear his suit, this was a small parachute that released the moment both triggers were held in simultaneously. Grandad really did think of everything down to the last detail.

He was now finally ready for the test flight of his rocket boots.

Who knows what amazing adventures he could have with these boots,

on a Monday he could go to the snowy mountains of Antarctica and by Friday be relaxing on a sunny beach in Australia, the sky is the limit.

The

Test

Flight

On the top of each lever was a trigger device and the left side was the throttle, depending how hard the throttle was pressed would determine how fast or how slow the rocket boots would propel the pilot. Grandad switched on the rocket boots: there was an on/off button on the left boot, he pressed it on, there was a sudden growling noise coming from the rocket boots, they were ready for take-off.

"Here I go Jimmy, stand well back," Grandad shouted, Jimmy backed up and gave Grandad plenty of room.

"Okay Grandad, good luck," Jimmy shouted back.

Grandad pulled the left hand trigger button, Grandad could feel the power beneath him as the rocket boots powered up and then huge flames came out the bottom of the rockets boots and launched Grandad high into the air, he then eased up on the throttle and began to slow down, the steering was all done with how you positioned your legs, in simple terms, position your legs to the left and the rocket

power of the boots will steer you to the left,

position yourself to the right… I think you

get the picture.

Grandad seemed to get used to controlling the rocket boots very quickly and so he should, he did design and build them after all. Grandad was enjoying every minute of his rocket flight, this is my best invention yet, Grandad thought to himself. Charlie, Betty and Tina were still busy picking fruits in the forest and could hear the roar of Grandads rocket boots as they all looked up they could see Grandad flying high into the air, as he glanced down, he could just about make out his tiny Topplelite family waving back at Him.

"This is incredible," Grandad shouted, going even higher into the air and was now heading towards Wishing Well in the forest, but there was a problem, the rocket's power was starting to fail? next there was a loud BANG! and Grandad started to plummet towards the wishing well forest at a lightning speed. Jimmy ran down the hill after hearing the loud noise and could see that his Grandad was in trouble, Jimmy made his way to the Topplefruit forest where his family were and they had heard the loud noise too.

"Grandad has crashed landed in Wishing Well forest, I hope he had time to use his safety parachute," Jimmy thought worryingly.

"Let's all go to the forest, Grandad may need us," Betty shouted.

So, they all rushed over to Wishing Well Forest and hoped that Grandad was all right.

Grandad had managed to execute his parachute and it broke his fall quite well, apart from he had crash-landed down the Wishing Well.

The wishing well was roughly about fifty-foot deep and five-foot wide and according to the Topple legend it granted wishes; the only wish Grandad would want right now is to not be stuck down this large damp well.

It was very dark and the only light was coming from the top of the well, Grandad, struggling to see, unattached the parachute from his suit and rolled it up to make a cushion he could sit on, he might as well get comfortable because he didn't know how long he would have to wait for help. There was no way he could climb out of the well because it was so slippery, so all he could do was sit and wait patiently for help to arrive. Meanwhile the Topplelite's all jumped into Charlies car and drove as fast as they could to the forest,

On the way over the bridge they saw Captain Scampi.

He was the local fisherman and a great friend of the family who was sorting out his morning catch, which looked to be a huge assortment of fish. Charlie stopped his car on the side of the road near Scampi's fish house, this house had been built by Scampi to look like a big blue fish, he wanted a house that stood out and everyone in the land would know where the local fisherman lived. Charlie wound his window down to talk to Scampi.

"Scampi, its Grandad he's crash landed in wishing well forest," Charlie shouted out.

"Mind if I jump aboard, you might need my help," Scampi answered.

"Not at all, let's go," Charlie replied.

So, Scampi got into the back of the car and off they all went to the forest, when they arrived, Charlie parked the car at Grandads house as from there it was only a short walk to the wishing well.

Once they were in the forest everybody started calling out for Grandad, then a loud-echoed voice could be heard saying" HELP, I'M DOWN HERE," it was coming from down the well.

"Dad, Grandads down the well," Jimmy shouted at the top of his voice, everybody was now crowding round the Wishing Well.

"Grandad are you alright?" Betty shouted down the dark well.

"Yes I'm fine, the parachute on my rocket boots saved my life, at least that worked," Grandad echoed back.

"We are going to get you out as soon as we can, Dad," Charlie said.

So, Charlie and Scampi went to get some rope and torches from Scampi's fishing boat,

while Betty, Tina and Jimmy stayed by the well and kept Grandad calm as they could.

Meet King Horn and his Men

King Horn and his minions are of the Hornite family, (basically this means they have all been born with at least one horn on their head) and they all live in the tallest and biggest building in Toppleland, which is a horn shaped castle and as you might have guessed is called Horn Castle. It has been built on a huge hill with a small gravel road circling the hill to the top where the huge main wooden entrance doors are located, all around the castle are lifeless trees and thorny bushes.

This is a place where all manner of horrible creatures lived, this includes, bats, snakes and very large spiders, not a place you would want to have a vacation, I can tell you!

King Horn's main objective is to rule over Toppleland and the people that live in it.

King Horn has two faithful servants Obo and Drax, they are his bodyguards, they are twin brothers and main difference between them is,

Drax has two horns that point upwards and Obo has two horns that points downwards. Obo is not the brightest of the bunch and very clumsy he is always tripping over and breaking things, much to the annoyance of King Horn but if either of them should get into any bother, they are both armed with large wooden spears, at the end of these spears are sort of half-moon shaped blades, basically if your caught by one of these it's going to hurt a lot, believe me.

King Horn has a mine under his castle where his devoted mineworkers dig all day for precious gemstones, these are cleaned and shaped and given to King Horn, he has built up quite a large collection over the years.

No one apart from the Hornite family has ever been inside Horn Castle, I'll be honest I don't think many of the locals would want to either.

King Horn has many people working for him in his labyrinth of mines that are located beneath the castle. The mines are supervised by Hornet and Ox and they keep King Horn updated with the daily movements and how many gemstones have been located.

The trains are constantly in use pulling along many trailers, there can be a lot of these running at any one time, the trains take trailer loads of gemstones to the sorting bays where they are sorted by size and colour,

the biggest stones are usually used to decorate King horns sculptures in his Jewel room, this room is in a secret location in Horn Castle and only King Horn knows where it is and can only be accessed by a password code.

King Horn relaxes in his throne with his pet

Snake Morton by his side.

Discovery

Captain Scampi and Charlie return with two rucksacks full of equipment, inside was a first aid kit, some strong long rope, two torches and some emergency snacks and sandwiches. Scampi tied the rope to the nearest and strongest tree and dropped the rest of the rope down the well.

"Joe, I'm coming down," shouted Captain Scampi.

Having good first aid skills he thought it best he went down the well first to check out Grandad.

So armed with a full rucksack and his torch

in his mouth,

off he went climbing down the well, followed

closely by Charlie, his torch shone against

the grey and brown bricks of the circular

well, revealing very moist and damp looking

bricks, they both descended even deeper

into the well.

"Grandad, you're very quiet, are you all

right?" Charlie said worriedly, but there was

no answer. Scampi had reached the bottom

of the well now and as he shone his bright

torch around it seemed as if Grandad had

vanished off the face of the earth.

"He's not here," Scampi said bemused.

"That's impossible, he couldn't just vanish into thin air," Charlie replied, who was now on the ground as well.

"We only talked to him five minutes ago, he said he had found something and needed to check it out," Betty said confused.

Tina and Jimmy were worried about Grandad, so Betty gave them a big hug.

"Don't worry kids, your Grandad is as tough as old boots, I know he'll be alright," Betty said, hiding her own worry.

Captain Scampi continued to search by torchlight when he noticed a gap in the wall, it was certainly big enough for the average Topplelite to fit through.

"Your Grandad must have gone through that hole?" Scampi said.

They both knelt down and shone their torches through the dark hole, on the other side seemed to be a tunnel of some kind, but where it led to was a mystery to them both. A small amount of light could be seen at the end of the very long dark tunnel.

"After you Charlie," Scampi said, guiding him through the hole.

"This tunnel should lead us to Grandad, shout up and tell the others that we are going in search of Grandad and we have to go immediately, there's no time to waste" Charlie replied.

So, Scampi shouted up to the others and told them the situation and then they both made their way down the dark and damp tunnel not knowing where it would lead them.

As they walked along the eerie tunnel all manner of bugs and spiders scattered about the walls as their torches lit up parts of the tunnel. Betty knew that in times like these they should go and talk to the Wise Tree, he lived in the forest just a short walk from the Wishing Well, maybe he could give them some wise words and friendly advice.

The Wise Tree

The Wise Tree was the most knowledgeable

being in Toppleland not to mention the

oldest, but then again trees do live for

hundreds and hundreds of years.

The Wise Tree was unlike any tree you

have ever seen before, he is very intelligent

and reads many books, especially ones

about medicines and potion making. He has

very long branchy arms that he uses to pick

up various fruits that he plucks from his

head, he then puts the fruits and other items he has foraged into his large wooden cauldron.

He crushes and mixes them all up with a giant wooden spoon to help create various medicines and remedies, these are then used by all the local Topplefolk and also visitors from further afield would come and for his help.

The Wise Tree was probably the closest thing Toppleland had to a doctor, if you had anything from a headache to a fever he would be able to make you a medicine or remedy for it.

Betty, Tina and Jimmy walked up to the wise tree who was busy as usual, reading from a potion book and mixing up some herbs and mushrooms up into his cauldron. Betty explained what had happened to Grandad and that Charlie and Scampi were in search of him.

"Knowing your Grandad, he found the hole and the curiosity was too much for him, so he must have gone inside to see what was in there.

I did not know of any tunnels linking up to the Wishing Well, but my guess is that it leads to King horns mines, as to who dug it is anyone's guess," said the Wise Tree.

"What do you think we should do now?" Betty asked.

"I would say go home for the time being as you all look very tired and have a little rest, something to eat and go back to the Well in the afternoon to see if there are any improvements on the situation, I'm sure Scampi or Charlie will report back as soon as they have Grandad," the Wise tree replied.

"Thank you, Wise Tree," Betty said.

Then Betty, Tina and Jimmy left the forest

and made their way back home.

The Mines

Charlie and Scampi were now getting close to the end of the tunnel, both wondering where it would lead them next? When they finally reached the end of the tunnel there was another small opening, Scampi and Charlie knelt to look through and see what was within it. Inside was King Horns underground mines, Captain Scampi and Charlie both turned off their torches as there was adequate light ahead in the mines, there were many glowing lanterns hanging up randomly on the walls, so they could see perfectly.

This was a huge area which consisted of a network of fast moving railway trains driven by the workers, these were thundering past with trailers full of mud and rocks and to the left and right were many tunnels which led to probably even more digging sites, the whole area was structured with heavy duty, giant wooden beams, probably to stop the whole area caving in.

Scampi and Charlie noticed a mine cart go past in the distance with what looked like Grandad in it, even from a hundred feet away you could tell it was Grandad, there were two guards with him, but because of how far away it was no more detail could be seen. One thing was for sure they needed to rescue him.

"What shall we do, Scampi, they've got my Dad," Charlie said really worried, with that they both had a great idea and jumped into the next mine cart that passed them heading in Grandads direction, luckily they both landed in the cart perfectly. The mine cart took them into a random tunnel, the cart thundered along at quite a speed, it seemed like only a few minutes and they came out of the large tunnel and then they could see the guards taking Grandad into a lift.

Another train thundered past them carrying what looked like jewels in amongst other debris.

"Charlie, Let's take a closer look?" Scampi said, with that they both jumped out of the mine cart they were in and made their way across the muddy-floored area across railway tracks, checking to make sure they were not seen, lucky for them there wasn't many mine workers in this section just the occasional train passing by, the main guards for this section had just led Grandad off into the lift. When they both reached the lift they noticed a control panel, it said "PRESS BUTTON FOR FLOORS" so scampi pressed it,

then dragged Charlie round the side of the lift in case the lift was occupied.

When the lift arrived they heard the doors open, PING! the lift doors opened suddenly, it sounded like the lift was empty so they both walked round to the lift doors, they were right, the lift was empty, so they both got in the lift and looked at lift control panel, this one had floor numbers with descriptions next to them, they were as follows;

PRESS BUTTON FOR FLOORS

Floor 6 -   **Bathrooms**

Floor 5 -   **Sleeping Quarters**

Floor 4 -   **Dining Room/Kitchen**

Floor 3 -   **The Throne Room**

Floor 2 -   **Storage Areas**

Floor 1 -   **Circle of Cells**

Floor 0   **The Mines**

Intercom

And at the bottom was an intercom button

that when pressed would mean you could

talk straight to King Horn in his throne room,

now that wouldn't be a good idea would it!

Charlie and Scampi were pondering over

which floor to go to?

"The Cells must be where they are taking

Grandad, let's try there first, Scampi said,

he then pressed the black button on the

keypad for the Circle of cells.

Circle of Cells

The Circle of Cells is the next floor up from the mines and is where King Horns mineworkers live as they use these cells as living and sleeping quarters. They work many hours at a time digging through the hard mud and rocks searching for precious gemstones, they need to keep the King happy as they wouldn't want to get on the wrong side of him would they.

Inside the large circular shaped room there are many prison cells that have all been built into a circle and are patrolled by a pack of vicious horned dogs that will attack any prisoners that try and escape the cells,

but the only prisoner in the cells at this time was Grandad, all mineworkers were safe from the horned dogs as they knew they worked for the King.

The mineworkers can work up to as many as twelve hours a day, digging for precious gemstones, can you imagine how hard it is to be constantly digging with a big heavy pick axe or shovel for that amount of time, very hard I can tell you, sore… blistered hands, aching back pains and constantly feeling tired, it's not the best life.

In each of the cells is a bed, a sink and a toilet, all walls are concrete built with a lockable sliding metal barred door.

Either Hornet or Ox checks the cells every couple of hours to make sure that the prisoners and horned dogs are ok.

Charlie and Scampi stood in the rumbling lift as it made its way to the Circle of Cells. There was a loud PING! then lift doors opened, there in front of them both was a pack of horned dogs, dribbling and growling at them. If you can imagine a Doberman pinscher dog with a green coat and two sharp horns on its head, then that's pretty much what it looked like.

"Select another floor quickly," Charlie said, panicking.

Scampi without hesitation pressed a random floor level on the lift display, then the lift doors shut just as the dogs were about to jump and attack them.

"Phew, that was a close one, those dogs looked like it was going to eat us for dinner," Charlie said.

"Well, I don't scare so easily, as you know I have been a fisherman since I was a child and there's not many sea creatures my dad and I haven't had chasing us in our fishing boat, Great white sharks, poisonous Sea snakes and even a gigantic Octopus, so, I laugh in the face of those dogs" Scampi replied.

Scampi was about to go into one of his infamous sea tales,

when Scampi realise that the random button

he selected in the rush to leave the circle of

cells was in fact King Horn's throne- room.

"That was not the best floor you could have

chosen," Charlie said.

"Well at least we're away from those dogs,"

Scampi replied.

With that the lift doors went PING! And the

doors opened immediately!

The Confrontation

King Horn sat comfortably in his jewel-encrusted throne, stroking the head of his pet snake Morton who was laying on his lap. His ever-faithful servants, Obo and Drax were standing either side of him and the keepers of the mines, Hornet and Ox were next to the lift, Charlie and Scampi came out of the lift and face to face with King Horn, who was sitting directly in front of them in his large jewel encrusted throne stroking his pet snake Morton's head.

The Throne room is a large circular room with many large marble pillars and attached to these were flaming lanterns, the main entrance to the castle was to the right of them, King Horn was just sitting and watching their every move.

"Where's my dad?" Charlie asked angrily. King Horn seemed to enjoy seeing Charlie in a worried state.

Calm down Charlie, he's in the circle of cells, we've made him quite comfortable," King Horn replied. "You better let him go, or else." "You are not in a position to threaten me as I hold all the cards, you must understand that I am a

businessman and a very successful one at

that and although my mineworkers work

very hard to dig and find me the biggest and

best gemstones,

I will always want more, I just feel I can push

production up a few paces by knowing

exactly where to dig, this would save a lot of

time and effort and make me a lot more

money." King Horn said.

"But what's that got to do with my dad."

Charlie replied.

"I need your Grandad to build me a gem

locator,

so I know exactly where to dig,

by the way how did you get in my castle? If

there's one thing I hate its trespassers."

King Horn said Angrily.

"You really think I'm going to tell you."

Charlie replied.

"Actually, no I didn't, but I thought I'd ask all

the same, anyway that makes no difference

to what I have planned for you." King Horn

said grinning.

"And what might that be?" Charlie asked,

trying to hide his fear.

"Scampi will be released as I have no use for him now and your Grandad will have two days to build me my machine, if this machine is not brought to me within this time, then you will be imprisoned here for a very long time, maybe we'll become good friends over time." King Horn said then stood up from his throne, Morton fell to the ground and slithered off to the side of the throne where he curled up into a ball.

"Mark my words, we will never be friends as long as I live." Charlie replied Angrily.

"Listen, it's very simple,

if I get my machine in two days, you will be freed, Hornet, get his dad out of the cells and lock up Charlie in his place, Captain Scampi you can go free." King Horn snapped back,

as not to anger or annoy King horn in any way Scampi thought it best to keep quiet and leave.

"Drax, open the main doors, and let Captain Scampi out," King horn said loudly. Walking out the main castle doors Scampi now just hoped that Charlie was going to be okay, thinking positive was the best thing to do and getting

Charlie out of there was the main objective for him now.

Two Days

Back at the Topplelites family home Betty,

Tina and Jimmy were getting ready to make

their way back to the well to see if there was

any sign of Grandad. Then there was a

knock on the front door, Jimmy ran to the

door and opened it, and there was Captain

Scampi and Grandad looking quite upset.

Scampi sat the family down in the living

room and they both explained to them what

had happened.

"So, if Grandad makes this Gem Locator within two days, Charlie will be freed," Scampi said.

"I think I can just about do it," Grandad replied.

"But what if your gem locator malfunctions, like your rocket boots did, King Horn will probably keep Charlie locked up forever," Betty said, now starting to worry about Charlie's safety in the clutches of such an unpredictable person.

"You will just have to have faith in me, I'm not going to let down my son, I better get back to my workshop, because time is ticking," Grandad replied.

So, Grandad went off to his workshop, Betty, Tina, and Jimmy stayed at home and prepared dinner. Scampi went to see a good friend in Toppleland.

With only two days to build King Horn his machine, Grandad certainly had his work cut out so Scampi thought it best to have a back-up plan which would need the help of Birdy Williams.

Birdy Williams is a big multi-coloured bird, with an even bigger personality, he is a very lively character indeed, most mornings he would fly off to see relatives from all over the lands and when he returned home in the afternoon, he liked nothing more than a dance in his tree house, which was on the east side of Toppleland next to the river. Birdy loved to do two things, fly and dance, I will be honest when it comes to flying, he is up there with the best of them, but his dancing is not so good because he is completely out of rhythm to the music, but I suppose if he is having fun, that's good enough for me.

Scampi went back to his fish house, once there he got in his fishing boat and headed down river to Birdy's Tree House. Scampi tied his boat to the river bank and as he walked he could hear some music nearby, this was a good sign that he was home, he walked through an opening in the woods to reveal Birdy's Treehouse. There was Birdy dancing to his music on the balcony of his Tree House jumping up and down and wiggling about, completely out of rhythm as usual.

"Hello," Scampi shouted.

Birdy turned the music down and stopped wiggling about.

"Hey Scampi, good to see you buddy, just having a bit of a dance," Birdy replied.

"Yeah, I can see that, I need to talk to you." Birdy flew down from his balcony and they both sat down on the thick green grass and Scampi told him everything that had happened. Scampi had a plan that was basically to get into the castle using the tunnel in the well and sneak Charlie out.

"Well, what do you think?"

"The thing is Scampi, being multi-coloured, I think I'm going to stand out a bit."

"Good point, maybe the Wise Tree can help us with that."

So off they both went to see the Wise Tree, which wasn't far from Birdy's house.

They made their way through the woods to the clearing where the Wise Tree lived, they could smell a most unusual fragrance that was wafting its way out of the Wise Tree's mixing bowl. It was far from unpleasant, just very unusual and was making both Birdy and Scampi feel very hungry.

"What is King horn up to now," the Wise Tree said.

"Well, he has imprisoned Charlie in the castle and wants Grandad to build a Gem Locating machine in two days, if this is not done on time he will keep Charlie locked up forever," Scampi replied.

The Wise Tree was mixing up a mysterious concoction in his cauldron, which was what they could both smell as they came in.

"We have got a plan and it is to sneak into the castle and get Charlie back, as we think the King will keep Charlie locked up even if he gets his machine, also Birdy being multi-coloured may get us

spotted a little too easily in the mines,"

Scampi said.

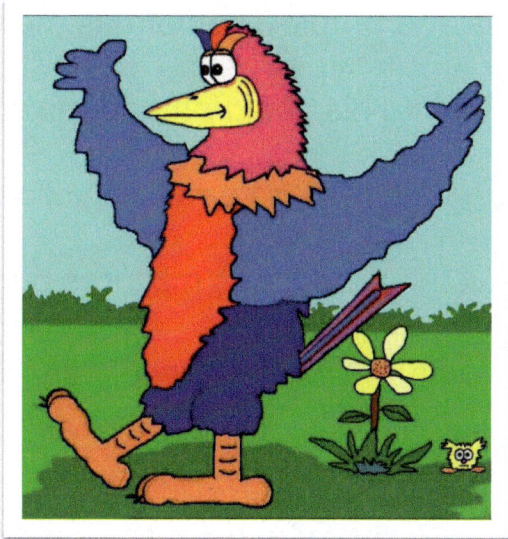

Blending In

The Wise Tree started pulling a variety of things from his head, like small leaves, branches and purple Topplefruits, he then put all this into his cauldron and mixed it up until the whole mixture turned a yellow colour, all the wise tree's mixtures gave off the most interesting aromas that would waft their way around Toppleland.

"Now then Birdy if you want to blend in, you must wash with this concoction I have just made, it will turn all your feathers yellow," the Wise Tree said.

"Okay if I must, but I've already had a wash today," Birdy replied, frowning.

Birdy started to wash with the mixture in the cauldron and as he did the colour from his feathers slowly changed to yellow.

"AAAHHHHH.... my colour, my colour has gone," Birdy shouted out.

"Calm down Birdy, it's only temporary and being one colour should make you stand out less, anyway when you return from the castle, I will give you back your full colour," the Wise Tree said, trying to reassure him.

"Okay then, but I'm going to have trouble getting used to this, as yellow is just not me."

The Wise Tree and Scampi found this hilarious and started laughing out loud.

"It's not funny, you wouldn't like it," Birdy said.

The Transportation Watch

Now they were nearly ready to face the

Castle, but they just needed to see Grandad

in his Workshop before they left, so they

made their way to his house. Grandad was

drawing up some rough plans for the Gem

Locator in his Workshop, the doorbell rang

suddenly, Grandad answered the door to

Birdy and Scampi, they then make their way

into his basement workshop.

"Birdy Williams, that colour really suits you,"

Grandad said, chuckling.

"Well, I don't like it at all, but it's part of our plan, so I can blend in better when we go into the castle mines," Birdy replied. Now starting to see the funny side of his situation.

"Joe, we have come up with a back-up plan just in case you cannot make the machine within the two-day deadline," Scampi said. Scampi goes on to explain their back up plan and how they plan to get Charlie back. Grandad walks to the corner of his Workshop and picks up a little wooden chest and puts it on a table near Scampi and Birdy, he opens the mini chest and inside is what looks like a Wristwatch and a black shiny cube, he places both of them next to the wooden chest on the table.

"This is going to help in your rescue attempt, it's something I invented a few years ago but kept it secret, I thought I would wait until the right time to show it to you, I call it the Transportation Watch. You put the watch onto your wrist and it's electronically linked to the black cube, then when the red button on the watch is pressed you will be transported to the black boxes location, wherever it may be, the thing is you can only transport two people maximum, the wearer holds the hand of the second person and they are both transported to the boxes location," Grandad said excitedly.

"So that means if we left the box here, when we get into the castle to rescue Charlie, we could transport ourselves back here to safety," Birdy replies.

"See that's the problem as you can only transport two people at the most, the third will have to make their way back by foot, also be aware you can only transport within a limited range, the mines to outside the Wishing Well would be fine, any further than that may not work?"

Scampi and Birdy thanked Grandad for the Transportation Watch and they both made their way to the Wishing Well.

Scampi was still wearing his rucksack with his equipment in it, he fastened the Watch to his wrist and put the Box inside the rucksack, he also realised that he still had loads of tuna sandwiches in his bag that he made earlier using some of his fishing catch from earlier that day, but with everything going on he felt this wasn't the best time to stop for a picnic, so he ate one of the sandwiches straight away to keep his energy up.

"Birdy, do you fancy a tuna sandwich?" Scampi asked.

"No, I'm okay, I've got some food of my own," Birdy replied, with that he put his feathery hand into his feathery belly area and pulled out some Topplefruit's, then started to tuck into them.

"MMMMmmm, tasty," Birdy said, biting into the delicious fruits, which caused all the multi-coloured juices to run out of his beak.

Imprisoned

King Horn was celebrating in the Throne

room with Obo and Drax, his pet snake

Morton was curled up snug on King Horns

lap and he was looking very comfortable

indeed, they were all drinking wine from

jewel encrusted goblets and Obo must have

had more wine than he could handle as he

seemed to be spilling his drink a lot and

falling into everything.

King Horn had two reasons to be

celebrating,

the first was he had his gem locating

machine being made by Grandad and

secondly was he had Charlie imprisoned in

the Circle of cells.

King Horn love's his gemstones more than

anything in the world so the more he could

own the better, if he could get all of

Toppleland folk to work for him in his mines

this would be a dream come true. He

actually has no intention of letting Charlie go

and as soon as Grandad returns with the

machine he will be lock him up too.

King Horn really needs to be taught a

lesson,

doesn't he? The problem is he doesn't just want to be the King of Horn Castle he wants to be King of Toppleland.

Charlie was sitting on his bed in his cell, watching one of the Horned Dogs that was outside the door staring back at him, it was watching his every move.

Each cell was about Ten- Foot square, they had a bed, a washbasin and toilet, the cells also had a second use and that was a sleeping quarters for the mineworkers when needed it.

Charlie seemed to be the only one in the cells at this particular time, maybe most of the workers were still digging for gemstones. The horned dog was now making his way towards him, sniffing the floor as he came closer.

When Charlie was put in the cell he was given a bowl of soup a crusty roll, he hadn't touched it so thought he would feed it to the dog,

he pushed the bowl of soup and the roll under the iron bars of the cell and watched the dog scoff the lot in a matter of seconds, the dog then just sat watching Charlie, licking his lips constantly, although the dog looked quite docile.

Charlie refrained from putting his hand between the bars to stroke him, as he thought it was likely to feast on it.

It has been said that King Horn feeds Sproglin's to all his Horned dogs.

Sproglin's are small, very cute furry creatures that live in and around Toppleland, they are all different colours and characters, most of the residents of Toppleland have at least one as a pet, including Charlie, his Sproglin is light blue and called Momo.

Maybe by feeding this Horned Dog his soup and roll, he hoped he might be saving the life of a Sproglin.

The Rescuers

Birdy and Scampi arrived at the wishing well, Scampi then attached the rope as before and they both descended down the Well. Once they were both in the tunnel, Scampi had to pull birdy through the small hole in the wall that led to the tunnel, it was a tight squeeze but he got through, then he led the way shining his torch in front of them both, Birdy did not like the dark, damp tunnel and the fact that they may bump into King Horn at any time made him quite nervous.

"We are nearly at the entrance to the Mines," Scampi said.

Birdy noticed another hole was very small.

"Scampi, if I knew I would have to fit down all these small holes I would have skipped breakfast," Birdy said Laughing.

"I'll go first make sure the coast is clear," Scampi said.

"Okay," Birdy replied.

Scampi climbed through the small hole and the coast looked clear.

"Right, go through head first and breathe in,"

Birdy squeezed into the hole that was a little smaller than the first one, everything seemed fine until he tried to get his stomach through.

"AAAAHHHHHH, I'm stuck," Birdy shouted.

"SSSSHHHHHH, someone might hear you, don't panic, I will pull you out," Scampi replied calmly. Locking hands with Birdy's, he pulled him with all his might, then all of a sudden he seemed to pop out of the hole like a cork from a bottle!

"PHEW! I thought I was going to be stuck there forever," Birdy said.

"Right, follow me, let's head for that mound of earth over there," Scampi asked. Scampi led the way and Birdy ran close behind, they both knelt behind a large mound of earth. The mines were made up of a network of railways so the workers could move large amounts of earth easily.

A train driven by one of the workers trundled past with three trailers, two of these were full of mud and rocks and the third was empty. This gave Scampi an idea, he got the Transportation box out of his rucksack and threw it into the third empty trailer.

"Hold onto my hand, I'll transport us to that empty trailer," Scampi said.

"I don't like the sound of this," Birdy replied.

Scampi pressed the red button on the watch, ZZZAAAAPPP!

They vanished from their current position and a second later were transported to the empty trailer and being taken into a dark tunnel.

"Where are we going?" Birdy asked.

"We need to get to the lift access area, it's through the other side of the tunnel" Scampi replied, picking up the Transportation Box and putting it into his pocket.

The train made its way out of the dark

tunnel and to what looked like a Gem

sorting area, full of mineworkers sorting

through the mud and rocks, searching for

gemstones. The train stopped, Scampi and

Birdy ducked down into the trailer,

two of the earth filled trailers tipped

sideways onto a conveyor belt and emptied

their loads for the workers to sort, as they

ducked out of sight in the trailer, they could

both feel their hearts racing. The train pulled

off again to the relief of both of them and

then it headed back onto another track to

the lift access point.

Once Scampi saw the lift, he threw the Transportation Box as near as he could to it and then transported both to of them to the entrance doors,

ZZZAAAPPP! once there they left the box where it was, as that was part of the escape plan for Charlie.

Scampi and Birdy got into the lift and selected the Circle of cells floor, once inside the lift made its way upwards, PING! the doors opened. "Scampi, jump on my back quickly," Birdy shouted.

Scampi quickly jumped on his back and then Birdy stepped out of the elevator, the horned dogs spotted them and they all started to run at them snarling and barking. Birdy flapped his wings and lifted off the ground and into the air at a rapid rate, the dogs were now under them barking, Scampi unfastened his Transportation Watch and threw it into Charlie's cell.

"Put the watch on Charlie," Scampi shouted.

Looking rather confused, Charlie did as he was told.

"The watch will transport you to safety,

just press the red button and it will transport

you to the mines, we will meet you by the

tunnel entrance to the Well, you know where

it is," Scampi shouted.

"Okay, I know the way back, see you soon,"

Charlie replied.

Charlie pressed the button,

ZZZZZAAAAAPPP, he vanished.

"Now let's get out of here," Birdy shouted.

With that Birdy flew into the elevator,

squeezing in just before the doors shut, the

horned dogs looked quite shocked,

maybe they hadn't seen a big flying yellow

bird before,

they just sat outside of the lift snarling at

them, the doors closed, and they both

headed down in the lift to meet Charlie in

the mines.

What they didn't know was King Horn was

on his way down to the mines with all his

guards, one of the mineworkers must have

seen Captain Scampi and Birdy creeping

around the mines then reported it back to

the King.

King Horn was close to getting into the lift

but before he did he turned to face a small

wooden cabinet on the wall, he opened the

door and inside it was a small lever,

he pulled it down.

"let's see how they deal with this," King Horn

said, then laughed very loudly for about two

whole minutes.

The lever had opened a secret door in the

circle of cells, it was an emergency slide

down to the mines, so the dogs could

quickly get into the mine works and chase

away potential intruders that might be trying

to take King Horns gem stones.

Escape

Scampi and Birdy stepped quickly out of the lift and started to run towards the tunnel by foot across the muddy, uneven ground, jumping over the occasional train track, behind them they could hear the sound of a pack of dogs barking loudly, they both glimpsed back to see the ravenous angry dogs hot on their heels, Scampi had a great idea?

"I've still got a load of tuna sandwiches and snacks in my rucksack, this should distract the dogs," Scampi said, with that he emptied the entire contents of his rucksack onto the floor as he ran.

The dogs which were all running behind them randomly then smelt the tuna fish sandwiches and all dived onto the them in a mad feeding frenzy, giving Scampi and birdy some vital breathing space as they ran along as fast as they could, they heard the ping of the lift doors opening, it was King Horn and all his main guards Obo, Drax, Hornet and Ox.

"There they are, don't let them escape," King Horn bellowed.

All his guards ran after them, luckily they had a good lead on them, the dogs had finished all the randomly scattered food now and had even eaten all the wrappers as well, they were now back onto chasing after them again,

"We are in deep trouble, we have King Horn and his men and all the dogs are getting closer, Birdy," Scampi said, running as fast as he could.

As they made their way out of the tunnel they could see Charlie at the tunnel entrance, he could hear all the dogs barking so he then climbed into the tunnel making his way to the Wishing Well.

"Just keep running, we are nearly there," Scampi replied.

Scampi climbed through the small hole into the tunnel leading back to the well.

Birdy squeezed through the gap and Scampi help pull him through with all his might, the dogs were close and heading towards the tunnel entrance at a fast pace, but they still had to climb out of the well yet.

Charlie was now climbing the rope out of the well and as he did he was greeted by his family who had been there waiting for their return, the dogs were all charging down the tunnel towards at a rapid speed,
snarling and growling as they ran along and had their sights locked onto Birdy and Scampi.

At the top of the Well, Charlie, Betty, Tina, Jimmy and Grandad were all now looking down the well, worried about the fate of Scampi and Birdy.

Scampi and Birdy climbed through the hole to the well and grabbed onto the rope for dear life and they both started to climb as fast as they could, the dogs were right on them jumping up as they climbed, one dog bit onto Scampi's shoe as he was climbing, it's teeth sinking through his leather boots but before the dog could do any damage he kicked his leg out and the dog fell on top of the other dogs at the bottom,

making them angrier than before, they reached the top of the Well and were pulled out to safety by Grandad and the family.

"It's good to have you all back," Tina said smiling.

All of a sudden they could hear shouting from down the Wishing Well, they all looked over into the well to see that the guards were climbing up the rope after them and the dogs and King Horn were at the bottom, looking up.

"Guards get them, they are my prisoners, don't let them get away" King Horn said Furiously.

The Guards were now getting very close to the top of the well.

"Leave this to me, Scampi said, pulling out a pen knife from his pocket and frantically started cutting the rope, as he did a hand from a guard came up to grip the side of the well,

then…SNAP!!! the rope gave way and all the guards fell down the well onto King Horn who was looking up the well, AAAHHHHH.

"That was a close shave Charlie, but you're a free man now," Scampi said.

"Yes, it felt like I may have been locked up in that cell forever," Charlie replied in relief.

"Now that we are all safe, I really need to see the Wise Tree as soon as possible so I can get back my colour,
I've felt like a totally different bird all day as yellow really isn't my colour" Birdy said.
Charlie and Scampi, Grandad and the rest of the family found this hilarious and all started to laugh out loud.

Celebrations

There were high spirits all round, especially Betty, Tina and Jimmy as they were glad to have their Dad back safe.

The Wise Tree gave Birdy back his colour which made him so happy he got his record player from his Tree House and started singing and dancing to his favourite music, this got everyone into fits of giggles, Grandad was telling Scampi about a new invention he had thought of.

Betty and Tina set up all the food, which included cakes, sandwiches and drinks, these were arranged in true picnic fashion so that everyone could help themselves. Charlie and Jimmy poured out glasses of Topplefruit juice for everyone to enjoy. Even the Sproglin's were joining in the fun and started jumping off each other's heads and doing somersaults. It was still very warm, so Betty and Charlie sat by the lake and put their feet in to help them cool down.

Toppleland was a Happy place again, but for how long, sorry to put a dampener on the ending but you know as well as I do King Horn will be back.

King Horn riding his trusty steed

The End

BONUS QUIZ PAGE

Okay, hope you enjoyed reading this book, how many of these questions can you answer correctly?

1) How many Sproglin's are there in total in this book?

2) What is Captain Scampi's house in the shape of?

3) What item helped break Grandad's fall in the well?

4) What colour did Birdy Williams feathers get changed into by the Wise Tree?

5) What sort of stones does King Horn collect?

6) What is the name of Obo's brother?

7) What is the name of the Topplelites family's pet Sproglin called?

8) What is the name of King Horn's pet snake?

9) What did Charlie feed the Horned Dog in the cell's?

* All answers are on the back page! *

If you enjoyed this Book you may

like,

Three Purple Mice

Free to read on Amazon Kindle

Unlimited and the printed versions are

available to buy on the Amazon

website.

About the Author,

I was born in Dunstable and have lived and worked in the area for most of my life, I enjoy lots of creative Hobbies including writing story's, drawing, painting and have just recently got into publishing my own books.

Answer's to the Quiz are:

1) There are 11 Sproglin's in this book.

2) It's shaped like a fish.

3) The Parachute broke Grandad's fall in the well.

4) Birdy's feathers were change to yellow.

5) King Horn Collect's Gemstone's.

6) Obo's brother name is Drax.

7) The Topplelite family Sproglin is called Momo.

8) King Horns pet snake is called

Morton

9) Charlie fed soup and a roll to the

Horned dog.

Thanks for reading,

Meet the

Topplelites

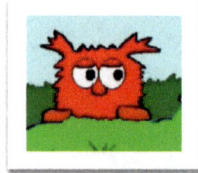